Get 30+ Patients in Under 30 Days

By Following Fast and Easy-to-Implement, Real-World Business-Savvy Techniques. Don't Let Your Competition Read This Before You.

Dr. Joe Simon

ISBN: 1484044924
ISBN-13: 9781484044926

DEDICATION

For my girls, Sophia and Lily.

ACKNOWLEDGMENTS

There are so many people that I owe thanks and gratitude towards, from my professors in college to my mentors in my professional life. I want to acknowledge my amazing staff for the support that they provide each and every day to keep the practice operational.

I would like to give a special acknowledgment to all the coaches in my life. From those who guided me in my early years of playing sports to the later ones who helped me in my career and my "other " business education.

Without their guidance and networking I would not have achieved so much so quickly.

The support of my family of is what has kept me on my quest to strive for perfection. I could not have asked for anything more.

FOREWORD

It will probably come as no surprise that in our twenty-four years of teaching doctors how to become more successful, we have found that the highest-earning practices are the ones that understand how to get a constant flow of new patients. It's as simple as that – you put a reliable system to attract new patients, you treat them well, employ solid business principles, and guess what? You will succeed!

The biggest problem is that we as health care practitioners never had the proper training in marketing to really do it right. We studied hard to make it through medical school, dental school, physical therapy school, optometry school, or chiropractic school, but we were never given the best tools to attract new patients.

So we compensate for our shortcomings. We read journals and books. We travel near and far to attend seminars. We try experimenting on our own, hoping to hit the right formula that will ultimately open up the floodgates to bring in the patients by the busload. But it rarely happens.

Why? Because there is so much misinformation out there. The marketing that worked even five years ago is not necessarily working now. Business is tougher than it's ever been.

But don't worry. Your life is now about to change.

We are not sure how you found this book, but it doesn't matter. You found it and you have started to read it and that is all that counts at this point.

Our colleague Dr. Joe Simon, a nationally-known coach to healthcare professionals, will guide you through the process of getting more new patients than you could ever imagine. The title of the book says you will get: 30+ New Patients in Under 30 Days. We actually think that is understated. Let's just say if you read this book carefully and put Dr. Simon's suggestions into place, your practice will be busier and more profitable than you have ever seen it.

Throughout the book, along with his great new patient strategies, Dr. Simon gives you clickable links to more references as well as bonuses. We strongly suggest that you click through to see what is waiting for you. And pay close attention to "Today's Prescription" at the end of each chapter.

There is more usable information in this one book than you would likely receive from any other source out there. If you take it all in, live it and breathe it, there is no question that you will see tremendous success in your quest for new patients.

So make sure you are in a comfortable setting with no distractions, and get ready to begin your journey. Let us offer you a big congratulations in advance for taking this important step in your professional career. Here's to your new patients!

Dr. David M. Madow and Dr. Richard H. Madow

"The Madow Brothers"

Chapter 1 – The Power Of Persistence

Most physical therapists and many other healthcare professionals feel that their skills will speak for them. The fact of the matter is that no matter how much your patients love you and think that you are the next big thing, as soon as they walk out of your door, they will forget you. Some of you may ask patients for a referral. Usually this is done at the end of their treatment sessions. Bad news. This is the worst possible time to ask for a referral. Why? If you ask a patient for a referral only once, it is very unlikely that a significant number of patients that will follow through. But if you ask for the referral earlier in their treatment (from their evaluation on) and then a second, third and fourth time, the percentage of referred patients will increase drastically.

The secret is to be at the front of your patients' minds when they need to make that referral to their friend, family member or coworker. This also is true for past patients. Keeping in contact with former patients will decrease the chances of them forgetting you and going to another practitioner.

Today's Prescription

What I want you to do today is build a list of all your patients: good ones, bad ones, those that were referred, those that only came once, etc. Once you have this list, you will write a follow up "How have you been feeling?" email. It should be short and less than a paragraph long. Each line should only contain six words across (this is to ensure the email can easily be read on mobile devices).

If you don't have their email address (though you should be collecting the email address of every patient), then a letter is fine. Then, make a note on your calendar to give them all a call one week later to see if they received your email. In this phone call, you will also schedule them for an appointment or ask them if they know anyone that might benefit from your services. As for the patients you are already treating currently, make it a point to ask them if they know anyone that could benefit from your services as well. When it comes to referrals, ask early and ask often.

The phrase "out of sight, out of mind" couldn't apply more here. So be persistent and those referrals will increase.

For more information and free bonuses, please visit,

www.privatepracticebusinessacademy.com.

Chapter 2 – Building Trust

Trust is the most essential ingredient for all relationships (in your personal life as well as your professional life). But trust must be earned over time. The only way to speed that up is to have someone vouch for you and your business. This is called a testimonial (and we will talk more about this later). To earn your patients' trust, you must keep your promises, follow through, and then remind your patients that you did what you said you were going to do.

This means not billing them for an extra amount after their treatment is done and sticking to treatment plans. If you tell your patient from the beginning that it will take twelve sessions to make them all better, then reevaluate them at the end of their treatment to show them the progress you have made and how hard you are working. When on the phone with a new patient that doesn't schedule, ask them if you can call back in twenty-four hours to make an appointment. When you call back as promised, say, "Mr. Jones, I promised you I would call back to get you on our schedule within twenty-four hours and I am keeping my word." You will be surprised how a simple act of trust will get those indecisive patients on your schedule.

Today's Prescription

What you are going to do today is train your front desk staff to return the phone calls of each and every patient that calls and does not schedule. Also, make it a policy that for each new patient seen or who has had a procedure completed, the treating doctor, therapist, or dentist will call that new patient in the evening to see how they are feeling after their visit. Trust is very important to your patients. They trust you with their health, so the least you can do is keep the promises you make to them and trust them in return.

Staff instructions: create a spreadsheet and leave it accessible for all staff members to update and keep track off. This way there will be multiple reminders to the treating clinician to complete that follow-up call by the end of the workday.

For more information and free bonuses, please visit,

www.privatepracticebusinessacademy.com.

Chapter 3 – Lost Patients? Never Again

Too many private practices concentrate too much on getting new patients despite the fact that old patients have a greater lifetime value. Former patients do not have to be resold on the benefits of your treatment or on how great you are. Sometimes they might have defected and gone to your competition, but they may not be as happy as they thought they would be. An effort to win them back could result in regaining a good customer and maybe even a referral of a friend or family member.

I remember a patient telling me, "Joe, my doctor told me to go to his therapist, and I have to admit, they didn't take care of me like you guys did. But I felt like a cheat and like I couldn't come back to you guys. Thanks for not giving up on me."

My trick is simple. I use the lost method of writing a "miss you" card with a short, personal note asking the patient how they are doing and if there is anything I could do to help. That's it. Short, handwritten and sweet. Even if the patient doesn't schedule with you right away, relationship-based customer service like this might encourage them to refer someone else. So don't give up on lost customers.

Today's Prescription

Ask your staff to hand you the list of all your patients you made the other day (from Chapter 1). You are going to send a "miss you" card to all patients that came to you more than six months ago and ask how they have been doing since you saw them last.

To take this a step further, use the now-famous Simon Three-Step Reactivation Campaign. I hinted at this in the previous chapter. The three-step campaign requires a lot of organization from your staff, but it is well worth the effort.

First, take your list of inactive patients and send them the card. After three days, send an email follow up to see if they received the card. On this step, you want to make sure to send an email to everyone, both active and inactive. The email will be a short message asking if they received your card. There are a couple of reasons to send this to everyone. Firstly, you want to make sure that you have the correct email addresses for everyone on file. Secondly, the people that respond to the email are your top 5% and will be your referral generators. With this technique, you are able to flush out the patients that care about you and your practice. The last step in the three-step campaign is a phone call. The phone call is only for patients on the inactive list that did not respond to the card or the email. In the case that they do not pick up, leave a short follow-up message.

This three-step campaign has generated as much as $26,000 for some of my private coaching clients. All it takes is some coordination with your staff and some sweat equity. Handwritten cards and phone calls show a patient that you care. Follow this protocol and you will keep patient losses to the bare minimum.

For more information and free bonuses, please visit,

www.privatepracticebusinessacademy.com.

Chapter 4 – The Other Four-Letter Word: "Sell"

I must admit, I am a marketing addict. I just love it. Once I found out how I could grow my practice with creative words and even small physical gestures (known as NLP – neurolinguistic programming), I was sold on those strategies. Most practitioners, however, hate the word "sales." They think it's beneath them. I hate to break it to you, but you sell your services every day.

Your patients must be sold on the importance and effectiveness of the treatment you are providing each and every visit. I will make this easy for you. I will hold your hand and show you step by step how this four-letter word will improve your bottom line.

The first thing I want you to do is put your business name on everything, including your contact info. There is no point in having a pretty logo if people cannot find you. Put it on your clipboards, pens, letterhead, envelopes, t-shirts, mugs, water bottles, wristbands, everything. The best strategy is to also include your website address on everything. Most people go online first when they do research, so make it easy for them to find you.

My former admin was out having a beer one night and talking to a beautiful girl. She wanted to give him her number, and fortunately for me, he didn't have his cell phone. But he did have a pen from the office, and when she saw the pen, she said she was looking for a PT office. He was more than delighted to give her the pen and our info. She became a great patient and they are still dating to this day.

Today's Prescription

Teach your staff that nothing leaves the office without your information on it. This includes the phone number, web address, physical address and tag line. Let the world know who you are. Do an inventory today of your business cards. Most physicians and healthcare practitioners in private practices worry about their logo. This is what I call a rookie mistake. You are not Coke or Pepsi. Stop trying to create a brand. Your business card should be your showcase. It should act like a small billboard. Both sides of the card should be used. Obviously, it should have the basic office information. Capitalize on the space on the back side. List all of the benefits of what your practice can do for the patient. The business card should not be a core dump of everything you might say about your practice; the aim is to present the reasons why a patient would choose your services and no more. So ask a few people to look at your new business card concept and take it from there.

www.privatepracticebusinessacademy.com
To check out some great examples of business cards.

Chapter 5 – The Ultimate Compliment

When was the last time you received a true, heartfelt compliment? I'm not talking about one from your mom or from your kids. For most of us, it's been a while. Well, the same is true for your patients. Compliments are rare. You see your patients one to three times a week, which means you have more chances than most anyone else to make them feel good about themselves.

When I used to work for someone else (back when I was a worker bee), I made it a point to connect with my patients on an emotional level. When they were able to accomplish a goal, I would make it a point to let them know what a great job they had done. And when they messed up, I took the blame as well and told them, "Don't worry; we'll do better next time. This happens to a lot of patients." Your goal should be to try your best to find a way to give every patient at least one compliment every time you speak to them. Beware of appearing shallow. Make sure to give sincere compliments. People know when you are being fake with them and they know the difference between a fake smile and a genuine one.

Today's Prescription

Your mission today is to give three genuine, heartfelt compliments to your patients. I also want you to meet with your staff and ask them to give three compliments to patients during each workday (not to the same patient). Also, ask them to stop asking how the patient is feeling. If they were feeling well, they would not be seeing you. Your staff should talk about anything else. Ask them to talk about how the weather is or about current events. Make it a point to ask them about work or their family. You will be surprised how people open up about their lives. Your staff will sometimes know more about a patient than you do, and when a patient feels known by the people who work at your practice, they will be encouraged to keep coming back.

For more information and free bonuses, please visit,

www.privatepracticebusinessacademy.com.

Chapter 6 – Sell Your Staff First

Can your staff tell you exactly what techniques and procedures you provide for your patients? Can they list the features and benefits of your treatments? A recent study showed that 86% of admin staff are unable to describe what physical therapy is outside of "It is a massage" and "The therapist is very good with his/her hands." It is amazing how dangerous hiring the wrong staff can be for your business. But what surprises me more is how little training most practitioners give their new hires.

In most hospital owned-physician's offices, the staff is hired by the hospital. The doctor has no control of who is answering his phones. This is a huge disadvantage hospitals are burdened with. But it's a huge advantage for private practitioners. Don't be afraid of being a manager. It's something we are not trained to do, but it has become a litmus test for whether a practice fails or succeeds.

If your own staff are not sold on your company, your mission, and your services and procedures, how will this lack of buy-in translate to their interactions with your patients? Training must be your first priority. My training process takes one to two weeks, depending on the position.

In The Ultimate Staff training Guide product, I show you how to guide your staff through the proper wording and phrasing from when they answer the phone to when the patient comes through the door for their first visit. This is taken directly from a series of trainings I created to train my own staff. That is how important I think this is, and I'd like to share it with you. We have videos and prerecorded messages on everything from the history of the company to where we project the company will be in future years.

For more information on the Ultimate Staff Training Guide, please visit www.privatepracticebusinessacademy.com.

Patients don't really care unless they see that you and your staff care. (This really pertains mostly to your staff because they are the first interaction a new patient has with your business.) Training and educating your employees will directly translate to increasing the patients' positive perception of you. A patient with a positive perception of you, your staff and your services is more likely to remain a patient, and more likely to refer others.

Today's Prescription
Here is an excerpt from "Training Admin 101":

Make it a point to have a set meeting with your staff once a week. In this meeting, go over the goals for the week, as well as any issues from the previous week. In this meeting, quiz your staff on the benefits of your practice. Benefits are the reasons a patient comes to you. It is not because you have the TX1000C piece of equipment.

If you don't know the difference between benefits and features, make sure to follow this simple rule: benefits are the reason a patient should come to you. Benefits solve problems the patients have. Features are the equipment or facility differences you have compared to those of your competition. Benefits are the most important thing. They are also the most difficult for most practitioners to pinpoint when I ask them what the benefits are for their facility.

In this meeting, I want you to practice reciting the benefits with your staff until it is second nature to them. If at any time a patient asks them why they should come to your facility, they will have an answer faster than anyone else. Having a knowledgeable staff will increase the conversion rate of prospects to patients immediately. But to do so, you need an informed staff.

Here are some examples of benefits used by my staff when someone calls for an appointment. This is said without prompting:

"We want to maximize your time at our office, so the best way to do that is to download the paperwork from our website or app."

If the patient doesn't have access to either, we ask if they would like us to fax them the paperwork. The goal of this is to show them we want to spend more time with them getting face to face time with the doctor, not filling out paperwork. And the staff will make sure to mention this to the patient while on the phone. It is a very subtle benefit that is hinted to the patient but something they will not forget.

Let me give you an example of a hypothetical doctor and a list of benefits and features he provides:

Dr. Paul Smythe has been practicing dentistry for over twenty years (experience is not a benefit, its a feature). He uses an X35J scope and x-ray device (not a benefit). He is able to see same-day emergency patients (benefit #1). Dr. Smythe's staff files all out of network claims for the patient (benefit). He does a free dental clinic for family and friends on the weekends (benefit #2).

These benefits show the patient different reasons why Dr. Smythe is a good choice. He files paperwork, he cares about your family and friends, and he is able to be there for emergencies.

There are some basic features in the example above, but they are of much lower value to the patient than the benefits. Here is a technique I use myself. Take a poll of all your patients and ask them what they like and enjoy about their experience at your facility. Everything they say will be a benefit, and it's a great place to start.

For more information and free bonuses, please visit,

www.privatepracticebusinessacademy.com.

Chapter 7 – Quality Speaks To Everyone

Quality is the cumulative effect of many choices. It is only after you make decisions that force your staff and company toward superior quality that you can communicate your goals to your customers.

Quality is a word that gets thrown around a lot in the world of basic marketing lessons for any health and wellness practice. If you take a look at company slogans, I would bet that eight out of ten of them have the word quality in them. The customer is so immune to that word at this point that they just plain ignore it. So what can you do to stand out?

Is it spending more time with each patient? Is it providing your patients with educational pieces at each and every visit? Or is it by keeping a finer quality of brand names in your washrooms for client use? In my experience, it is all of the above. Patients want to spend time with their practitioner even if it is only for five extra minutes. Providing your clients with material that will help increase their understanding or make it easier for them to explain their condition to a loved one will make them feel more informed about and included in their treatment and set you apart from the rest.

Most practices keep their bathrooms clean, of course, but they fail to provide a brand-name hand wash, face wash or clean towels (and I don't mean paper towels). Something as simple as the presentation of your bathroom will have your patients saying good things about you like, "That is probably the nicest bathroom I have ever seen; it's nicer than mine!" for months to come. One of my patients, Diana, spoke about our bathroom so much that her husband came by one day just to see what all of the fuss was about. He later became a client for our training program.

Today's Prescription

There will always be patients that appreciate you going that extra step. Those are the patients that have no problem paying a premium for your services. The people you want to form the core of your patient list. Your task today is to work on the benefits of your office and practice. I want you to write ten benefits and ten features of your practice. Don't copy someone else in your profession. Instead, I want you to look outside your profession to get some examples. As a matter of fact, I want you to look outside the healthcare industry for an example. We touched on this a bit in the previous chapter, but I also know how difficult it was for most of my coaching group to wrap their heads around this, and so it is worth revisiting. It is also one of the reasons I am dedicating multiple chapters to understanding why a patient should choose you over their competition.

For more information and free bonuses, please visit,

www.privatepracticebusinessacademy.com.

Chapter 8 – Technology Is Your Friend No Matter What Your Age

My mom is sixty-nine years old and just started texting and using Facebook on her new smartphone. She tried to resist it for years, saying that there is no way she could figure it out. She said she would just like to remain an old lady. (Not my words; I love my mom very much.) Well, once she spent the time to learn, it was amazing how fast she has adopted other pieces of technology in her day-to-day life.

How many practitioners (including MD's, PT's, OT's, dentists etc.) have basically shut down their practices due to the ever-changing face of technology in healthcare? By the time you buy a new computer or piece of software, it's already out of date. There is an updated model coming out just around the corner.

Despite the frustrations involved in keeping

your equipment and software current, technology equals improved productivity, which in turn makes you more competitive. Having a budget set aside to update your technology yearly or quarterly will help you increase your productivity, and your customers will notice that you are on top of the very latest equipment innovations, which in the end will make their lives easier.

Let's take for example a scanner that I purchased for my staff. Did we already have a copy machine in the office? Yes we did. But with the scanner, we could copy pages front to back and send it directly to their computers. They no longer needed to go to the copier, wait for it to warm up, make copies, and then mail the pages to the patient. The time alone saved with this new, streamlined process has made my staff more productive, improved our response time with patients, and saved me thousands of dollars.

Today's Prescription

What I want you to do today is to work on the intake process for a new patient in your office. Start with the phone call. What time are the majority of your patients calling your office? Is it a time when you are not in your office? Is it when your staff is overwhelmed with patients? How can you use technology to help streamline this process? Do your patients have the ability to schedule online? What about an online, live help desk to answer their questions? I could list hundreds of examples of how today's technology can make your office more efficient and provide a better experience for your patients. I myself have used www.ringcentral.com for all of my call answering needs. They have been great at streamlining all the phone numbers with multiple offices.

www.privatepracticebusinessacademy.com to check out what other companies I recommend to help streamline your office.

Chapter 9 – Inspire Those That Sail Your Ship

If you haven't purchased my product Training Admin 101 yet, I encourage you to click here **www.privatepracticebusinessacademy.com** and buy it now. Not because I want to make that sale, but because it will help you and your team to understand how important their role in the company really is. We want to inspire your staff, educate them, and above all, make your practice a success. Can you think of anything more important?

The real secret to inspiring people is to get them involved and to give them a reputation to live up to. Showing them exactly what is expected of them and how their role helps the company achieve its goals will prove to them that this is not just a minimum wage job. After all, if that is what they were looking for, flipping burgers pays well, it doesn't require much brain work, and they are always hiring.

Tim, the owner of a PT practice in Gainesville, Florida once hired two receptionists and had them trained by two different people. One was a staff member that had been working for him for years and the other had been working there for less than a year. Tim thought that if he split them up, he would be able to train the new employees faster. To Tim's dismay, the admin trained by the seasoned employee picked up a very bad work ethic and expected that this was the norm. She was often late, didn't complete tasks on time and worst of all, displayed a very carefree attitude towards her job.

Unfortunately, Tim had to fire the new hire, but he also let the seasoned staff member go as well. Why? When he recognized the staff member's poisonous attitude toward the business, he had no choice. His first reaction was, "I wasted all those years, afraid if I let her go I would not be able to replace her." His practice doubled in productivity once she was gone and he realized that he had to make better management decisions in the future.

Today's Prescription

To avoid this, give your staff members the proper training they need, but also give them a goal to live up to. They will own that and make it an inspiration for themselves and others to follow. People become what they see themselves as in their mind's eye. When you lift them up and put them on a pedestal, they will perform at that level.

I have touched on this in previous chapters, but I want to dig deeper into what exactly I want you to do with your staff to help increase both motivation and productivity. In the past, I have put incentive programs in place and they failed because they didn't get to the core of why certain employees worked for me. Everyone is motivated by something different. Not all employees are the same. Money is not everyone's incentive.

Let's take for example my employee, Kim. Kim loves to get her hair done and have spa days. I make a spreadsheet of items I need done and give it to Kim. If she completes all of the tasks ahead of schedule, she receives a gift card from me to her favorite spa. When she goes above and beyond the tasks I give her, she gets an appointment at her favorite salon. She is working toward a goal specifically tailored to motivate her. She removes the stress from my daily activities and the price I pay for the incentives is absolutely worth it.

For more information and free bonuses, please visit,

www.privatepracticebusinessacademy.com.

Chapter 10 – Big Payoffs From Surveys And Suggestions

Sometimes a patient wants to express a concern or suggestion without getting anyone in trouble. A simple suggestion box for constructive criticism or a survey that is handed to patients could go a long way.

Let's take for example Dr. Mark Dolin, DDS. I advised Dr. Mark to send a survey out to his patients asking three questions. Each practice will be different, but the concept will help you devise your own questions. The questions on Dr. Mark's survey are below:

1. What one thing would make your experience at XYZ Medical facility a more satisfying one?
2. Is there an employee you want to thank for their services? Why?

3. Are there any suggestions you can give us to make your experience a better one at XYZ facility?

The feedback was amazing. They were just simple questions that he had never thought to ask. One patient asked for a hook in the bathroom to hang her jacket up on. The small details make a huge difference. Another patient asked for a reminder email or call about when their next appointment would be. Now, most offices assume leaving a voicemail on a patient's home phone is the best way to contact the patient. I changed this procedure in my clinics by asking a simple question at the time of patient intake: "Mr. Jones, what is the best way for us to get ahold of you? Would that be by your cellphone or email?"

After his patient asked for a reminder of her next appointment, Dr. Mark made a simple list with email, cell phone and work phone contact information. He then had a new, multi-media format to stay in touch with his patients. A simple suggestion transformed his patient contact list.

From all of the suggestions Dr. Mark received, I created a marketing campaign that targeted all the details mentioned in the survey, which we emailed out to a list of 750 clients at the cost of zero dollars. This yielded a return of ten patients and a 13% increase in new-patient referrals. And it was all because Dr. Mark cared for his clients' well being and followed up with them.

Today's Prescription

The more you can tailor your products and services to the wants and needs of your patients, the more likely they are to become long-term clients and provide referrals. Dr. Mark's example is something we can all learn from. Today, create a simple survey and have your staff hand it out to all patients. Make sure you have a stamped self-addressed envelope attached to it. You want to make it easy for them to return the survey to you.

If you have your patients' email addresses and have an email list, I suggest surveymonkey.com. They are a great site that lets you create all types of survey templates. I have myself made several surveys and I have noted the fun and quirky ones get an even greater response.

With the advice we received from the surveys, we were able to create two new programs just for patients.

For more information and free bonuses, please visit,

www.privatepracticebusinessacademy.com.

Chapter 11 – Being Creative With Your Advertising

Too many times I have seen practitioners copy the advertising of other private practices word for word and simply insert the name of their own business. This is called "me too" advertising, and it does not benefit anyone. The average person on the street does not have a clue about what you do. To use my own practice as an example, only 4% of people have an understanding of what physical therapy really is (and we are not talking about those people who say, "Oh, so you do massage?").

So what is the answer? How do you break free from common advertising traps and let the general public know what you do can help them without saying it in technical terms? That's where certain advertising techniques come into play. How many times have you stopped to read the funnies in the Sunday newspaper or in a magazine? Chances are the answer is "a lot," and that is because cartoons grab attention.

Can you take a comical experience that happened to you in the clinic and turn that into an ad? Here is a great example of something that we have used:

Training for the
Marathon?
We Can Help You Finish
Call Us Today–
800-555-5555

Using cartoons adds life and humor to your ad, which will differentiate you from everyone else. Yes, you are a medical practice, but don't think that anyone will think any less of you if you make them laugh. As a matter of fact, they might just get to see the human side of your practice and that very well could be what they needed to see. If you are reading this book and thinking to yourself, "I can't put a cartoon ad out there about my practice. We are serious about what we do and we want everyone else to take us seriously," then consider this: people will take you seriously because of your knowledge, expertise, and your staff's professionalism. But ask your employees which place they would rather work in – a serious one or one that is funny and engaging – and you'll begin to understand the power of creative advertising. Most people will assume you are an expert at what you do, but they will also assume that about the competition. The point is to differentiate your practice by allowing potential patients to see beyond your degrees.

Today's Prescription
So let's brainstorm and start creating. Here is a quick step-by-step method for you. Any time you create ads, try to start with the formula of a problem, solution and humor.

The cartoon ad you see above is a great example of this. The humor is the cartoon, but it shows a person struggling to run (problem) and the solution (we can help you finish). But how? Call today to find out. You want to pique their interest to call and also give them a direct command. You don't want to leave it to chance for them to call anytime. You want to make sure they call now.

Remember, if your advertising is like everyone else's, you will probably get about the same results they do. Break through the clutter and add a healthy dose of creativity and humor to get a better response from your ads.

For more information and free bonuses, please visit,

www.privatepracticebusinessacademy.com.

Chapter 12 – The Magic Trick

Most physical therapists, massage therapists, and even professional trainers want to know the one magic trick that will get orthopedics, podiatrists, and general practitioners to refer all of their patients to their practice. They are on an endless quest for the Holy Grail. The simple answer is that there is no magic trick. There is, however, an organized series of questions, responses and tactics you can use to get more referrals from physicians.

Charlie, a now-retired physical therapist, once taught me the simple steps needed to generate endless referrals from physicians. Even though times have changed, most of his principles still work today. In my Endless Physician-Referral Guide, I lay out the entire plan, step by step.

1. Find out as much as possible about the physician on a personal level to help build a rapport.

2. Probe, dig and unearth what the prospective physician needs.

3. When that picture is clear, you present them with the magic question: "If I can find a way to provide the products and services you need, would you consider referring your patients to me?"

It may be impossible to do this with every physician you want referrals from immediately. Building rapport takes time. This is a six-week to six-month process. My best analogy is going on a date. You wouldn't say, "Hi, would you prefer my place or yours?" on the first date. But if you build rapport first, take them out, get to know them, then within six weeks, your chances are going to be significantly higher.

Get to know the doctor. Believe in what he does. Show him why you do what you do. Send him patients. Show him that you trust him too and that this will be a long-term relationship, one based on trust. That is the magic trick.

For more information about my Endless Physician-Referral Guide, please visit www.privatepracticebusinessacademy.com.

Today's Prescription

What I want you to do today is to research five doctors in your area. Find out where they went to college, what hospitals they work at and even what information is on their website. There might be a fundraiser or professional event that you can introduce yourself at.

This technique works well for physicians that are looking to affiliate themselves with a powerful marketing group in the community. Finding out what the group needs and offering your services pro bono can build amazing relationships and will identify you as the go-to expert in your respective field. Now imagine if you could connect two groups of potential affiliates. I want you to take some time right now and brainstorm. Who can you connect with and who can you refer them to?

A great example comes from a pediatrician that was promoting his practice in conjunction with a health food store. The store was very popular and it generated great community relations with the school district. Dr. Stephens made a small informational packet about what foods created a greater allergic response and what to do if such an event happened. Dr. Stephens also helped at parent informational nights at the store. The store promoted its latest healthy food substitutes and the doctor became known as the go-to expert in the community.
Who would make a good fit for your practice?

For more information and free bonuses, please visit,

www.privatepracticebusinessacademy.com.

Chapter 13 – Networking

Dimitri, a young physical therapist, had tried several times to get past the gatekeepers at a prominent orthopedic group. Time and time again they were very polite to him, took his information and told him that they would add him to their list. Dimitri never even got the chance to speak with the doctor. He could not understand why the front desk would not just let him speak to the doctor for even a few minutes.

He knew that he could offer a better treatment program that could speed up the recovery process for certain types of ACL and RTC surgeries. But how could he get to the doctor to tell him that? One Sunday morning at the local playground where he played basketball, Dimitri overheard a couple of guys talking about the knee surgery one had had and about how great the doctor was but how bad the physical therapy sessions were. Never one to badmouth anyone, Dimitri just offered some free advice and guided them both through some drills that would help speed their recovery and build muscle.

After two weeks, Dimitri received a phone call from the doctor's office asking for his information. The patient that received the free advice happened to have had an appointment the following day and told the doctor that one session at the playground had been better than six weeks at the referred physician's office.

Today's Prescription (1)
So the question you have to ask yourself is: who do you know that can open doors for you? Appreciate the power of networking and giving without expecting anything in return. It can go a long way. People are always happy to tell someone about a great deal that they received. How can you use that to your advantage in networking and at your local doctor's office?

Here are some simple suggestions.

1. Ask more questions and listen to responses.
2. Know when to shut up.
3. Give to get is not the goal.

The mission is to do your homework. Find out who your colleagues, co-workers, friends and family know. Almost everyone knows someone else who could be a prospect. This is the key to networking.

Can social media expand your networking in your community?

Facebook is all the rage, but more than one healthcare practitioner has told me that they tried using Facebook for marketing their practice and it didn't produce any results. Let's see if the lines below sound familiar

1. I hired my daughter's friend to run our social media. She is really good at it and it costs me only a couple of bucks.
2. I don't want to add another gadget or gizmo and waste my time when I could be doing something much more valuable.
3. I don't know how to use Facebook or "Tweeter."
4. I spent money on Google AdWords and it was a waste of money and time.

These are the most common kinds of remarks heard from many in medical field when it comes to social media. Lets go over this. No matter how great it sounds to get cheap labor and how awesome you think your kids are, they are NOT the experts, and if they are, the last thing you want to do is damage control when they accidentally tweet something from your account after they have been partying till 4 a.m. on a Saturday night.

Today's Prescription (2)

You are right: you yourself should not be wasting time on setting up your social media campaign, but you are the person that must donate content and your knowledge to the page. Setting up a page and having a member of your staff update it on a regular basis with your knowledgeable content is how you should do it.

BUT DON'T BE BORING. Do you think people want to read about a root canal or how your ACL patient was able to bend his knee to 45 degrees today? Not unless that patient happens to be a local celebrity (who you would have to ask permission to post anything about).

If you can make what you do informative and FUN, then by all means create a Facebook page and update it regularly.

I want to give you a great tip (my inner circle of mastermind private practice owners might be a bit upset), a SECRET TIP that increased our patient load in twenty-four hours. I wrote a great article about sitting posture, put in some FUNNY pictures and gave some great tips on how to strengthen your back to avoid pain in a post on our Facebook page. There was a small button asking if I wanted to promote the post for $5. I clicked yes. It was sent to everyone on our fan page, plus their friends, plus all of our contacts in the email account associated with our Facebook page. We had a bunch of likes (which don't mean that much) and twenty-three shares (which means a lot). We also received three phone calls to schedule ergonomic consultations and five new patients that all were suffering from back pain. $5 created a huge return on investment. What can $5 do for you?

Would you like me to walk you through that Facebook promotion step by step? Go to www.privatepracticebusinessacademy.com for more information.

Chapter 14 – Why Should I Come To You?

Recently, I have been working with a physician's group to help with their marketing. They built a brand new surgery suite, have a pristine office space and state-of-the art equipment. But when I asked them the simple question "Why should I come to you for treatment?" I didn't get a real answer. I can't believe that the entire group thought that just building a new surgery center would be enough.

I have done a lot of consulting and my fees are enormous, but they wanted me to give them that answer. I told them, "I was just hired; you guys should know your own business."

The truth is, most private practice doctors have a difficult time explaining what they do in thirty seconds or less. I mean explain it clear enough that your target market would understand and schedule an appointment immediately after speaking to you. You must put yourself in the position of the patient. Go to another doctor's office and be a patient. Go through all the steps. What is it that you dislike about being a patient? That will be your first clue.

Today's Prescription
But the doctors that hired me didn't like that answer. They spent a lot of money on the new surgery center and wanted answers immediately. They wanted me to wave my magic wand and generate paying patients from thin air. So I gave them a step-by-step marketing plan._

Here are a few steps:

1. Why does your patient need you?
2. What are your patients' wants? (Yes, there is a difference between needs and wants.)
3. How are you different than everyone else out there? (And please, don't talk about yourself.) This is the 200 million dollar answer.

For more of the steps, please visit us on Facebook at

www.facebook.com/
PrivatePracticeBusinessAcademy.

The patient wants to know how all your skills and fancy equipment will benefit them. What benefits warrant them choosing the treatment you offer that is different from everyone else? Also, make sure that your staff knows this answer. Nine times out of ten, your staff is asked this question and not you.

You (and your staff) must be able to explain to the patient in the simplest way possible how you can make them better, healthier, stronger, and get them back to their normal life activities. That's what makes you different, and if you answer this question and your staff knows the answer as well as you do, you will be light years ahead of your competition.

Quick tip: Create a cheat sheet for your staff and keep it by their phone. This way, if they are on the phone and need to answer this question, they can do so immediately.

For more information and free bonuses, please visit, www.privatepracticebusinessacademy.com.

Chapter 15 – Asking For Help

As I stated in the previous chapter, the physicians' group sought out and secured a deal to obtain my help. Too many times, I have seen doctors, therapists, and dentists too proud to ask for help, thinking that they could do everything by themselves. I am going to reveal something about myself here. I was exactly the same way. I thought that I could do it all on my own. That was pride or stubbornness. Either way, it was wrong. Modeling yourself after someone that is successful is the first step to becoming successful, but asking for help and committing to hard work are as important.

Most practitioners (and I am going to target physical therapists here) go it alone, and when they search for help, they stray too far from the profession to help give them the real answers. Asking other therapists was not easy in the past. But today, with the help of social media and the change in the mentality of therapists now wanting to further the profession, I have seen a change. There are also a few guides in the physical therapy niche, in addition to strategy companies that provide advice, though those generally do not exclusively focus on physical therapy.

Today's Prescription

My advice is simple: don't blame anyone else for your problems, and don't reinvent the wheel. The key is to learn from someone that has already done it. Asking for help will keep you from making the mistakes that others have made. For more information on my private coaching program and business consultation, please contact me at,

www.privatepracticebusinessacademy.com.

What has private coaching done for me? It has changed my life. I was probably just like you: I figured I had all the answers. My wife called me stubborn, and she was right: I did not take the time to see who else I could learn from. And when I finally did sign up for private and group coaching, the learning was amazing. Not only did I have a group of people just like myself. (I have to admit that most people don't like talking to me about marketing or sales strategies, so for me it was like I had found a second home.)

For more information, please visit www.privatepracticebusinessacademy.com.

Chapter 16 – Respect Their Time

We live in an age where people feel incredible pressure to get things done immediately, both in their business lives as well as in their personal lives. Let's take for example a coaching friend of mine in Minnesota. J.R. runs a successful medical and fitness facility. J.R. was on track to break gross profits of $500,000 in his first year of business. How was this possible?

J.R. realized that the biggest complaint people had about medical facilities was the time wasted waiting for appointments and during appointments. So he came up with a time-specific model that would benefit his clients. We streamlined his new-patient intake and gave his clients the option to complete most of their paperwork online prior to their visit. Once they came in, they were greeted and their "experience" at the facility began. We were able to cut more than one hour and ten minutes from the average time of an office visit.

The patients' reaction was outstanding. They could not stop talking about their "fast and effective" visit to J.R.'s practice. So what can you do to help speed up your client's visit? Can we streamline the patient's intake paperwork so that it is not so confusing and time consuming? Can we direct new patients to fill out forms online? Can we create an experience that respects their time? (We will speak more about the "experience" in future chapters.)

In Front Desk Training, Vol. 1, I break down what patients expect from a regular MD, PT and dental appointment. It's not surprising what they expect, but it's shocking that the profession has been so late in addressing what patients don't like. Over the years, we have all been conditioned to wait for doctors, and that wait is one of patients' top complaints. Also, 95% of patients have reported that they were greeted by a rude individual that only told them to sign in and take a seat. With just those basic insights, we can see an excellent opportunity to tweak the patient experience and even change it entirely.

To view Training Admin 101, Vol. 1, please visit www.privatepracticebusinessacademy.com.

Today's Prescription

Identify the key areas in your practice where a sense of urgency is important. Make a document summarizing the information and show it to your staff so they can all maintain the schedule accordingly. Part of your research should include an appointment at a competitor's office. See how well or poorly they manage patients' time. By developing a sense of urgency that meets your patient's needs, you will show them that you care not only for their health, but for their time as well.

Years ago, I worked for a practice where patients were scheduled every fifteen minutes. If a patient were late or early, I would have three patients to see at one time. I can't tell you how miserable that made me feel. I didn't even have the time to give each patient the fifteen minutes allotted to them. I really only had minutes. The reputation of that practice suffered because the patients correctly perceived that the practice did not value their time. When the economy changed, they were unable to show their patients why they should keep coming. They had already established themselves as the bottom feeders for patients who were looking for a good deal, and when they lost patients, those left (who were paying sub-premium rates) were not enough to keep them afloat. People are extremely value-conscious, but it's a mistake to assume that the only value they judge you on is cost.

Do you want patients that are booking for competitive pricing for their healthcare? I don't. So establish yourself as different by creating a superior experience, one that patients will rave about to their friends and family. Value your patients' time and they will value yours. This is a great objective to have, but very hard to live up to. As much as possible, resist the urge (the greed) to treat more than one patient at a time. Value their time and they will value yours and they will value the service (the experience) you provide.

For more information and free bonuses, please visit,

<u>**www.privatepracticebusinessacademy.com**</u>.

Chapter 17 – Do You Qualify?

In the last chapter, we spoke about what type of patient you want to visit your practice. And yes, we all want the patients with excellent insurance and the ones that pay their copay, so let's figure out how we can get that ideal patient. Most practices are doing what I would call playing defense. What that means is that they spend most of their time getting a patient from a referral or insurance plan and they spend the rest of the time treating that patient and every other patient that comes in. Again, it doesn't matter if it's their ideal patient or not. They're just playing defense. Nothing is wrong with this. Hey, we all have to pay the bills one way or another. But are you happy with that? Is your staff happy with that?

What I have taught a lot of my private coaching clients is playing offense by "qualifying" your patients. Yes, I said I want you to qualify your patients. Is it legal? Well, you are not allowed to abstain from giving life-saving treatment to anyone, but you are allowed to see the doctors, people, horses, etc. of your choice. You are allowed to fire patients as well. It's your practice. Don't let a bad seed bring down the morale of the entire practice. That said, let's get back to qualifying your patients.

Consider this process as turning everything you know on its head by qualifying your patients when they call. To make this work, you have to stack up the benefits of what your practice has to offer. If you believe you have nothing to offer them, please put this book down right now. You are in business to show why you are the best. And if you're reading this book, I am assuming that you already know how good you are.

Today's Prescription

So have those benefits listed. You might be able to get a patient to feel better in fewer visits with a certain technique. Make sure to let them know that, and at the time of their evaluation make sure to tell them, "Ms. Jones, with your diagnosis I am confident we will have you feeling better in four sessions. But I need you to commit to the entire program right now. If at any time you deviate from my treatment regimen or if you think this regimen is too tough for you to follow, then I would rather you see another therapist who can better accommodate you." This is how to qualify your patients.

You might be thinking that this is crazy. They will want to be accommodated as much as possible. Yes, it's true that I want you to accommodate your patients with excellent customer service. But when it comes to treatment, I want you to qualify them. This will help you segment your list of those that are dedicated to their health and those that are not. You want the patients with commitment, and they are the ones that will refer more patients like themselves to you. Also, they will be the type of patients you want to work with and your staff will want to work with.

Remember, the more exclusive an item is, the more people want that item. Compare the pricing of an iPad to that of a Kindle. Plenty of people buy Kindles, but even they wish they had an iPad. Make your patients want to be a part of your exclusive list.

Exclusivity might not be what you are thinking your practice needs when you are struggling to get patients. Trust me: I've been there. And a big part of the difference between when I was desperate for patients and now has been qualifying my patients. Remember, not everyone wants what you are selling, even though they may need it. That's why being an exclusive provider makes them want it more and gives you an easy way to not take on that patient that would give you and your staff a headache anyways.

For more information and free bonuses, please visit www.privatepracticebusinessacademy.com.

Chapter 18 – Email Marketing For Your Private Practice

Let's face it: email has become the most prominent method of communication in our society. Running a close second is text messages. It seems that the US Postal Service is feeling the effect of email. The sheer volume of letters has decreased, and soon, Saturday delivery will end. Even now, the post office is trying to combat technology when they should be embracing it. I'm not knocking them totally because they have some great programs that I use (I will talk more about that later).

But I can't tell you the number of doctors' offices I have consulted who all tell me the same thing: "We just started asking for email addresses of our patients, but not all the time." I usually want to hit my head against the wall and ask them what they mean by "not all the time." I feel like asking them, "Do you want your patients to pay you sometimes or all of the time?" By the time this book is finished, over 82% of people will check their email more than four times daily.

Let me give you an example of a chiropractor who asked me for help with his marketing. He was averaging over 275 visits per week. Nothing wrong there, I told him. His marketing was actually generating a waiting list. But he said to me, "Tell me, Joe, if I have a waiting list of patients and a waiting room filled with patients, why am I still struggling to meet my payments every month?"

Now, I am not an accountant, and I strongly urge that everyone have a good one in addition to a great billing manager to help you see to your intake and expenses, but for Dr. Mater, I took a quick look. The one thing I saw was that his collections and follow up with collections were costing him a lot of money. So I didn't change his marketing. I changed his collections schedule and the way he contacted his patients.

We created a three-step process. The first was a letter that went out in the mail stating the balance owed and the due date. The second was an email follow up asking if the patient had received the letter and if not, a copy of the letter was attached. The third was a phone call to let them know that they would be sent to collections.

62% responded to the letter and phoned the office. The next 20% responded by the second email. That is a whopping total of 82% collected with just the push of a button. The phone call captured 7% and at the end of the three-step process, we had about 10% go to collections. This is a big difference compared to what he was dealing with before. The additional income pushed his practice to the next level. He was able to expand and hire another doctor to help see the patients on his waiting list. This process is not specific to collections; email can be a powerful tool in all of the patient-contact elements of your practice.

As for email marketing, it is a great tool, but it should not be abused. Know what you are using it for. If you want to send out an email marketing newsletter, that's great. But make sure that you are delivering value and great content. Don't push your practice by just talking about yourself and how pretty your office looks.

Make it a point to deliver 90% content of value-based material (talk about what is new at your practice and how it could help the patient—focus on the benefits to them) and only 10% about other things. Email marketing is the key to attracting referrals from prospective patients. They may not be ready for your services now, but being on their mind at the right moment may just generate a new patient referral. The first step is to add an email contact line to your patient intake form. Make sure that the patient fills it out. If they refuse, tell them that your office sends reminders for appointment times and schedule changes only by email and that it is required. You will see that most people would rather have that done by email than receiving a phone call during dinner.

Going back to the email newsletter, the frequency of mailing is important as well. Mailing them only every once in a while will allow patients to forget about you. Once a month is okay, but again, we are trying to stay on their minds to get those referrals. What I think is a great starting point for you and my private clients is twice a month. When you build a good following on a bimonthly schedule, you can switch to sending emails weekly or even daily. It all depends on your goals and what you have to say.

Today's Prescription

Be sure you are collecting the email address of every patient and, if possible, every prospective patient. Use the list to deliver your bimonthly newsletter, to check in with patients about how they are feeling after receiving treatment from you, to remind patients of their appointment times, and to encourage on-time payment.

Respect patient privacy and never, ever share your email list.

For more information and free bonuses, please visit www.privatepracticebusinessacademy.com.

Chapter 19 – Staying On Your Patient's Mind

In the last chapter, we spoke about email marketing and how it keeps you in and on your patient's mind. Why is this important? Well, I am going to be brutally honest with you. No matter how much your patient loves you, as soon as they walk out that door, they completely forget you. People are busy. The average person is bombarded with over 5,000 images daily. On top of that, you have to add in their family and work lives, which will always be their top priorities. As soon as they are feeling better, they ignore you and even forget you.

Let's take for example the family practice doctor. Your kid gets sick and you take him to the doctor. The doctor examines him and gives him a course of antibiotics. Your child takes these for five days and usually by the third day, your kid is running around like crazy in the house and you have to struggle to get him to finish the medicine. But the doctor set a follow-up appointment for you. Did you know that the no-show rate for follow-ups is 76%, and the cancellation rate is even higher, close to 97%? So what does that tell you? You are only needed when someone is not feeling well. This is the same for PT, dental, etc.

In my PT practice, when someone starts feeling better, we see a rise in cases of "I got busy at work and need to reschedule". But when they are in pain, they don't care what is happening at their job. So what can you do to stay on your patient's minds? There are a number of things that you could do. Newsletters are always very useful. This could be in print format (which we do at my practice) or in email format. We also like to send gifts to our patients. Make sure it is not just during the holidays, but at random times also. I have a rule that what matters is not the price of the gift, but rather the value that the patient gets from it. Make sure that it is something that is related to them or the clinic. Make it remind them of the experience they had during their sessions with you.

Emotions are powerful tools in marketing. Make sure to use this tool wisely and sincerely. Follow-up communication either through email, a letter or a phone call is a great way to remind patients about your clinic and your services. It provides a way for them to think about how you helped them. I space this out every three to six months.

Remind your patients of the great experience they had with you by demonstrating your expertise and your willingness to help them. You will be surprised how many people will decide to see you if you can help them with something else or give them a referral to another doctor that works in an area outside your experience. In a previous chapter, I spoke of building a network and this is an excellent way to capitalize on helping your network grow.

Today's Prescription

Today's task is simple. Figure out what you can do to make your patient remember how great you are, and not only when they are sick, injured or needing dental work. Brainstorm three ideas and implement them with your staff immediately. Your first three ideas won't always be your best ones, but you can modify and improve your new system for staying on your patients' minds over time.
For more information and free bonuses, please visit, **www.privatepracticebusinessacademy.com.**

Chapter 20 – You Have To Smile To Work Here

There are only two kinds of employees that determine if you are going to get that new patient to continue treatment and refer more of their family and friends. The first are the people who are going to work for you, and the second are people who will never work for you. Ever. And it all comes down to the smile.

One of my best employees was horrible at learning the new scheduling software. She was so bad with computers that she cried every time the computer beeped at her. She hated her new Mac computer because she was a PC girl.

The only reason I did not fire her, and the reason why she became one of my best employees ever, was her smile. It was contagious. When a new patient came in to the clinic, scared, in pain and not knowing what to expect, her smile put them at ease and made them feel comfortable. Smiling is a simple act, but a smile delivers a powerful emotion to whoever it's aimed at. So we put more hours into her training for the new software and double-checked her work, and it was worth every extra minute. Because of that smile.

We also implemented a new campaign named the "smile campaign." When a new patient would come through the front door, the staff was instructed to smile and greet them. In turn, when the therapist came to see the patient, they were instructed to smile and make eye contact as well. Now you must be thinking, what if my staff is having a bad day and doesn't feel like smiling. NOT my problem! And not yours either!

When your staff comes to work and when they punch in, they should be ready to perform like a singer on stage. So whatever they have to do to get themselves pumped up to bring their energy level up is fine with me. I once had a therapist that would give himself a pep talk before leaving the staff room. He would gauge where his energy level was at the moment and say, "I'm at a four and I need to be an eight." Then he would walk out and perform with the best of them.

Today's Prescription

Have a team that understands that the simplicity of a smile is sometimes all a patient needs to start feeling better. Make this clear to your staff; they need to know that's it's not only good business, but that by smiling they are also helping the patient. So look into the mirror and practice that smile.

For more information and free bonuses, please visit ,

www.privatepracticebusinessacademy.com.

Chapter 21 – Please Call Me Sir

I once treated an elderly gentleman (Medicare) and I could not bring myself to call him by his first name. He was very kind and he insisted that I call him by his first name, however, I was raised to address elders as sir or ma'am. This was also the case when I worked for the Air Force, where it was reinforced tenfold. When I started working in a private practice, it took me a while to change my habits. But the respect I had for my clients did resonate with them.

The biggest problem I see with front desk staff is that they tend to skip formalities. They automatically address the patient by their first name. You must be thinking that this is really not a big deal, but let's take a look at a survey we had for a few of my consulting clients. One of the main objectives was to gauge patients' reactions to their front desk experience, specifically patients aged thirty-five to sixty-five.

The results showed that they were not happy about being addressed by their first name by a twenty-two-year-old girl sitting behind the front desk. They reported they felt that assuming first-name familiarity connoted a lack of respect, and that is what the patients remembered about the practice. Is that what you want to be remembered for? Don't give your patients any negative talking points.

Remember that a person's name is one of the most important things to their sense of identity and feelings of respect. Once they give you permission to use their first name, by all means, go ahead and use it. But it's important to wait for the invitation to do so. And please avoid the classic blunder of using a common nickname for long or hard-to-pronounce names. Ask the patient for help if their name is hard for you to say. They will thank you for it. And if they say that a lot of people mess their name up, make it a point to tell them what a great and original name it is. Complimenting someone's name will psychologically earn that person's trust and acceptance immediately. So get into the habit of asking permission and using patients' names the way they prefer them to be used.

Today's Prescription

Organize a staff training today. Go over how your staff should address your patients. Listen to the staff and see if there are any tips you can give them and vice versa. They may tell you that patient xyz likes to be called by a name that was not in their chart. Update the chart immediately and make sure to call them by the name they are most comfortable with.

For more information and free bonuses, please visit,

www.privatepracticebusinessacademy.com.

Chapter 22 – Are You Listening?

Asking the patient for correct pronunciation of their names means that you are listening. But did you know that most staff, including the professional staff of doctors, physical therapists and dentists, are often guilty of the crime of not listening? We are trained in the medical profession to look for "tells" and certain key words that will help diagnose the patient. And the majority of the time, we are guilty of just not listening to the patient's entire history.

I have witnessed it firsthand. I was shopping for a Jeep Wrangler (I love jeeps) and I wanted the metallic blue with a grey soft top. The off-road kit was additional, but I made sure to find a dealership with this in stock. I just wanted to go in and buy it. Well, when I got there, the salesman started with his pitch. I was polite and told him that I found the exact one I wanted and I wanted to simply buy it. He just ignored what I said and continued on with his pitch and asked me to get into a yellow CRV for a test drive.

For the non-car enthusiasts reading this book, even you will understand the difference in motives here. I just wanted to buy a jeep and he wanted me to test drive a CRV that wasn't even the right color. Was there a price difference? Yes. The jeep was probably more expensive because of the off-road kit. But this salesman could not see what he was doing. I was so turned off that I left the dealership and waited two days to make my purchase online. The salesman not only lost his commission from me, but also from my network of referrals that wanted to know where I purchased the car.

You can see how not listening to the patient can really affect not only the relationship between the two of you, but also the chance of future referrals and continued business. When it comes to listening, really listen and take mental notes on even the smallest details that your patient might mention in passing. A favorite restaurant, movie, weekend plans, etc. We use this information to buy them gift cards to their favorite places as a way of saying thank you for being such a great patient. (There are a lot of influences at play here and I will get to them in more detail in the next chapter).

Today's Prescription

When it comes to listening, make sure to take those notes and mention something the patient said to you at another appointment. They will be amazed at how someone actually listened to them. You must remember that most people go through their day with others telling them what to do, how to feel and how to act. So when they get a chance to vent and speak to a neutral person, it makes them feel better.

The average patient will judge their doctor by three things:

(1) A word of mouth referral,

(2) The plaques hanging on the wall with their degrees,

(3) And the most important thing: bedside manner. Meaning that you listened to what the patient had to say.

Here's an assignment I want you to do: every patient that you see, please jot down a quick note about their day, their outfit, anything they mention to you. At their next visit, make sure to ask them about it.

For more information and free bonuses, please visit

www.privatepracticebusinessacademy.com.

Chapter 23 – The Cash-Based Practice: Always Tell Patients What You Can Do And Let Your Staff Handle The Money

What I have seen lately is an increasing number of doctors, therapists, and chiropractors opting out of insurance plans. The ability to pay your staff, rent and various overhead expenses becomes increasingly difficult when insurance reimbursements decrease or are not being paid at all. There are many people talking about starting cash-based practices.

Easier said than done. Pricing will obviously be different than for in network reimbursements. But how can you convince your customers, clients and patients to buy from you? The average patient will be frustrated. They will become angry. That anger will be directed towards you and your staff. How you handle their situation will determine if your practice will be a successful cash-based practice. Let's go through the motions.

The first thing I used to do in the past was talk about how great I am as a therapist. How my facility is clean and how we have state-of-the-art equipment. I would spend the entire time talking about myself and the clinic. I wish that I could flash a giant warning sign here. Please do not do this. It is a huge mistake.

Patients do not care about the state-of-the-art equipment or how great you are as a doctor or therapist. **Patients care about only one thing: their health.** They care about how long it will take to get better, what they will have to do, and above all whether they have to pay out of pocket. So be sure to address all of these objections, complaints or concerns immediately. Do not try to cover this up. Be upfront and honest. Let them know you are not the bad guy. You are doing a job just like them, and your job is to get them better and you cannot do it without their help.

Tell the patient that you are unfortunately not participating with their insurance carrier BUT (this is the key word) that what you can do for them is create a cost of treatment based entirely on their budget, a treatment plan based on what they need to get them better as fast as possible. This is where your benefits and bonuses will stand out at your practice. And I don't want you to get scared with the wording here. This will be in the hands of your front desk staff. A properly trained front desk can make this process seamless. In my Front Desk Training webinar, I go through this in depth. I have increased the bottom line for multiple clinics by over 30K a year.

You can find more information about my Training Admin 101 program by visiting: www.privatepracticebusinessacademy.com.

I make sure to emphasize this part: you are the physician, therapist, or chiropractor: the healer. You are not to discuss money with the patients. Separate yourself from this position. This small move will solidify the relationship between you and the patient and they will look to the front desk as the place they have to discuss their financial stresses.

Today's Prescription

Remember to put yourself in the position of the patient. Address all of their objections before they can bring them up. And remember to give them the good news prefaced with the word "but" and the bad news first.

What you will do today is create a payment plan for all your services, breaking the payments into three or four-month cycles. Please make sure all patients that opt for a payment plan are billed on the same day every month. Otherwise it's an accounting nightmare.

For more information and free bonuses, please visit,

www.privatepracticebusinessacademy.com.

Chapter 24 – Perception Is The Key To Value

I wanted to follow up on that last chapter because it is so important to distinguish yourself as the healer and not as the financial bad guy. To run a successful cash-based practice, your staff must be able to further the perception that you can bring value to the patient's life. But often the staff talks about how great the clinic is and too often does not have any supporting facts or understanding of the benefits for the patient. Do not operate in the dark. Conduct surveys and get a true grasp of how your patients view you and the way they see the value you are providing.

This was an eye-opening experience for Dr. Neely, an optometrist from Connecticut. Dr. Neely has been a client of mine for about eighteen months. We decided to run a test and asked all of his patients (active and inactive) if they would help with a survey. In return, they received a discount coupon for a pair of eyeglasses.

The stories we heard were great, but what we found out was that his office manager would send bills out to all of the patients with a bad attitude, acting more like a collection agency than the contact person for a doctor that cared about his patients.

Now, I understand that insurance payments take time and we only find out after the fact what the coinsurance is. But is this method of collections done by most healthcare providers? Maybe so. But what are their patient loyalty numbers? That is a statistic that I am interested in seeing. Sending a letter to patients and asking them how they are doing is important. During the call, staff can also ask patients to call the office so that the billing manager can provide them a review of their insurance payment. Let them know the billing manager will be available to answer any questions they may have regarding payment. That wording alone will change the clients' view about your practice. From the patient's perspective, it's the difference between you trying to get something from them and you trying to help them with something that may be difficult for them to understand.

And guess what? When that patient is out with his or her friends and the topic comes up, your office will be described as amazing, great and courteous. All because you changed the wording on a collections letter. Treat others like you would like to be treated yourself. The Golden Rule has always worked for me and my business.

Today's Prescription
Go over your collections practices and mailings today and implement changes that will help your patients perceive your practice in a more positive light. To see a template that I use, go to
www.privatepracticebusinessacademy.com.

If you would like me to send you the exact paperwork that I use plus the wording that has helped keep my patients loyal and my collections close to 100%, make sure to fill out the order form at
www.privatepracticebusinessacademy.com.

Chapter 25 – The Patient Assistant

What is the patient assistant? Well, there are physician's assistants and physical therapy assistants, so why are there no patient assistants? What would that job entail? How could this small idea promote your office by leaps and bounds?

Let me give you an example that we can all relate to. Most people hate telemarketers because of the intrusion factor. Dinnertime calls give salespeople a bad image. So excellent sales professionals have learned that they should be more of a helper and not a seller. They started finding out what their customers' problems were and how to solve them. Using this approach, they were not looked upon as the bad guy desperate to make a sale, but rather as someone who was truly committed to helping people.

In your practice, the best salespeople are the people who (in the eyes of the patient) are on the patient's side. They find out what the patient's problems are (which usually has to do with insurance) and try their best to find a solution. Having a patient's assistant in your office is something that can be promoted and marketed very well to the general public. If you want to be different, find out what problems your patients are facing and let them know you have a dedicated staff member who is there to help.

Today's Prescription

Find out what frustrates your patients. Find out why they would rather go to a competitor and help them find someone who suits their needs. Be seen as the helper, not the seller. Always provide solutions, because you are the only practice with a patient assistant on staff.

You don't have to go out and hire a new person for this job. Rather, award it to the individual in the group that shows the most compassion and caring and who will also be able to guide the patients to make the right decision in being treated by your team at your clinic. Make sure your new patient assistant position is made available on all your media marketing channels, and even do a press release about it. You will be surprised by how a small idea like this has been so overlooked and how much it can do to make current patients happier and bring in new patients.

For more information and free bonuses, please visit

www.privatepracticebusinessacademy.com.

Chapter 26 – So What Makes You Different?

In the beginning of my career, people would ask me, "So what makes you different than the PT guy down the street?" I would answer with all kinds of B.S., because I wasn't prepared to answer the question in a way that set me apart from the competition. I would say that my patients like me (so what). I know some special techniques (so what). I have all these titles at the end of my name (so what). I get people better faster (okay, now I'm starting to listen). How? Then I would go back to the same B.S. lines that I said before. There are always things I did when I was just starting out that I wish I could change, and this is a big one.

The question is entirely legitimate, and I was answering it wrong. I should have been listening to what the client was asking for, and only then responding.

I was always too fast to answer and never really listened. I wanted to give a quick answer, so I just said whatever came to mind, the same kinds of well-intentioned things that the competition was probably saying. This was a bad strategy, because when you do what everyone else is doing, you get the same results as everyone else. That is usually bad or just below average. "What makes you special?" is a fair question, and it is one you should know the answer to.

Today's Prescription

So I am going to tell you a secret. This is a secret I usually reserve for those in my private coaching group, but I want everyone to implement something immediately from this book. The secret is to take a procedure that you do already, no matter how basic it is, and I want you to break that up into steps or phases.

An example in the rehab industry would be the treatment plan. We provide a comprehensive four-phase treatment plan that must be followed for three weeks with a follow-up week. Now, the norm in the industry is "go to physical therapy two times a week for four weeks." Which one looks and sounds more appealing? Which one demonstrates forethought to the patient? We have implemented this in a dozen facilities (all healthcare) and even our fitness centers. The results have been extraordinary.

You don't have to go by just my example. Let me tell you about the "describe and display" method used in many industries. The fitness industry already does a good job of this by breaking down your strength gains and nutritional changes over time. The plastic surgery and dermatology sectors of healthcare have some great examples of how to take a basic, everyday procedure, give it special terminology, and break it up into phases that will describe the treatment in a new light. The point is to make it clear to the patient what you will do for them (describe) and show them the results (display). It's excellent packaging of your product, and it helps the patient know exactly what they're in for and the value of the treatment once they're finished.

Recently, I held a workshop for entrepreneurs and a gym owner at the end of the day approached me and said that he wanted to use this method in his gym to show a significant difference between him and the competition. So we brainstormed for a moment and he told me all of the steps that a client goes through when they are signed up for personal training. We decided to rename this intake process the "6 Stages of Fat Loss and Muscle Gain XT." He was exited to report to me that a week after implementation, the sheer curiosity about this program increased sales by 18%.

In actuality, nothing had changed. It was the same routine that they had given their clients previously but with a new title and phases that even secured media coverage. So please take a look at the everyday policies and procedures. Giving them a new title and being able to present and explain them in a novel way might just breathe new life into your practice.

For more information and free bonuses, please visit,

www.privatepracticebusinessacademy.com.

Chapter 27 - Loose Lips Sink Ships

I believe this was a typical saying back in the early nineties. I'm also sure the term goes all the way back to WWII, but nevertheless, it holds very true for your practice to gain the loyalty of your patients. Most people assume that if they confide a secret to their doctor that no one will be the wiser. But in most practices, there are actually other staff members that are within earshot overhearing a patient's deep secret. I have seen this mistake happen not only in one of my clinics, but also when I went to a new podiatrist for a sprained ankle. (Yes, physical therapists can hurt themselves too. We are not invincible as most of my patients might think.) Let me describe the scenario.

I walked into the doctor's office and told the front desk that I was in for an appointment. The front desk girl, who was in the middle of a conversation with another team member, quickly gave me paperwork and got back to her conversation. A big deal to me. I just wanted to see the doctor and I could already see that the customer service was poor. As I was filling paperwork out, there was a section that required my credit card information. I just wanted to use cash and make sure that this information was only for my copay. As I approached the front desk, I could hear the girl talking about the doctor's private business (about an argument he had gotten in with a mistress who happened to be a patient). Very intriguing story. I wanted to hear more, but I really needed to ask the staff my question. As I cleared my throat to get the receptionist's attention, she looked at me and repeated to me to fill out everything. I asked her about the credit card and she told me to fill it out if I would like to.

By the time I saw the doctor, I knew his entire life story. I already had some pre-judgments about him. Needless to say, at that point I did not value his education, his authority, or expertise. And the ripple effect of a referral or partnership from my clinics (he did not know I was a PT) would never happen.

So talk to your staff today. "Loose lips sink ships" is as true today as it was seventy years ago. So don't let it be a true at your facility.

For more information and free bonuses, please visit,

www.privatepracticebusinessacademy.com.

Chapter 28 – Pile On The Benefits

When most practitioners talk about their office, facility, or practice, they do a lot of "me" talking. I mean that all they talk about is ME, ME, ME. They pile on the talk about new equipment, how awesome they are, blah, blah, blah. And this is exactly how it sounds to a prospective patient or client. To avoid this, make sure to also talk about the benefits of your service. Because in the end, that is what people are really interested in.

Here are three good phrases to start with:

1. What that means to you...
2. This is important to know because...
3. You will love this, because it will help you...

I heard a great example of this from a Dan Kennedy event. For those who do not know who he is, he is the Godfather of direct mail marketing. I am going to paraphrase this because I don't believe he has written down this article:

When people go to the hardware store to buy a drill, what are they really purchasing? The drill? The bit? Nope. You are really looking for something to create the hole. To create the hole is the benefit of the tool, and that is what you are really purchasing from the hardware store.

In my practice, I have always done some reverse engineering of my patients' wants and needs. That is, I find what they are looking for to get better faster. They don't want to pay surprise fees and they want to be educated about their condition, so I make sure to add this with my marketing. I make sure to say we can get them better faster, more effectively and we will educate them on their condition to help avoid this from happening again.

The key is to learn to become a great communicator of both your features and benefits. Your prospective patients will see that you are really giving value and they will want to become your client or patient. At the end of the day, people are not looking for products; they are looking for what that product, service and education will help them achieve and accomplish.

Today's Prescription

At your next staff meeting, brainstorm ways to present your services to patients in terms of patient benefits. Involve staff as much as possible in this, because they will generally be the first-contact point with patients and prospective clients.

For more information and free bonuses, please visit,

<u>www.privatepracticebusinessacademy.com</u>.

Chapter 29 – Pricing Too Low

This is an epidemic in my industry. As a physical therapist, we are considered healers. And we are kindhearted people (usually). When it comes to charging a person for our services, I can't tell you how many times I have heard someone say "Don't worry about it. I am happy you are feeling better" or the classic "I charge below what everyone one else is charging because I want my patients to be able to afford my services." These two comments have been destroying my profession.

I have consulted many therapists in the last two years. Many have advanced degrees and certifications, and some reading this book will disagree with the next statement: Raise your prices! Charging a flat fee or what you are used to receiving from insurance companies (usual + customary fees) does not measure your worth.

During a private coaching session, Pam, an occupational therapist and owner of Coral Hand Therapy, was adamant that if she raised her prices she would lose all her patients to the hospital or another private practice. So I fought tooth and nail with Pam. I told her to raise her prices by $5 just so that she would be the highest-charging occupational therapist in her area, even if it were only by $5. She did. Guess what? No one batted an eye. So after ninety days, we did it again, but this time by $20. We had a 7% drop rate. 7%! That's it. This freed up time for

Pam to spend working on her business and not in her business. The lost business was more than made up for by the increase in fees, and Pam was left with the best clients on her list. I want you to learn what Pam learned: you are worth more than you think.

Today's Prescription

So start small and work up. Keep going until you see a drop rate of 10%. Stay at that rate for ninety days and then raise your prices again. Now, you must understand that raising your prices and not offering more benefits doesn't work. That is called greed. Offering more in time, handouts, education, gifts, etc. will show your patients that you are worth the price.

Never let them question the reason why you cost so much. This is a great quote and I can't remember where I heard it, but I loved it: "If everyone was shopping based only on price alone, then everyone would be driving a Hyundai" (or whatever the lowest price car is these days). Don't think that your patients will automatically leave you because they can't afford it. People will figure out a way of affording things to get them better. Don't forget that they're not only paying for your services; they're also paying for the relationship they have with you and the service your office provides. If you have built that relationship, they will be happy to pay more, both because you're worth it and because they know that starting over with another doctor is full of unknowns.

A great example of this is my friend John. He was suffering from tooth pain for nearly two months. Yes, he waited for two months because he did not have dental insurance and he assumed that he would not be able to afford treatment. Suddenly, he woke up and the pain was excruciating. He was charged $300 for tooth extractions and some other work. He said that it was the best $300 he ever spent. Not only that, the dentist offered him a follow-up visit at a discounted rate and gave him an educational sample to take home to help keep it from happening again. My friend still talks about how great the dentist is and makes sure to tell everyone that he was well worth it.

Are you that valuable to your patients? Raising your prices might just make them believe you are. Give it a try. Start small and work your way up, then reassess your drop rate and the quality of patients you keep.

For more information and free bonuses, please visit,

www.privatepracticebusinessacademy.com.

Chapter 30 – Everyone Is A Doctor These Days

In today's high-tech, Internet-savvy mobile world, it is nearly impossible to know what a patient knows without doing some research. There are a lot of dangers in making assumptions. It's also dangerous to get caught up in the medical jargon and assume that your client knows what you are talking about. My rule of thumb is always start by "dumbing it down." If the patient responds with a solid working knowledge of your field or has medical knowledge of his or her condition, it is best to ask them what they know already. They might give you feedback on your own website or a new website or service you have not heard of. Work with them on this. Be that friend in medical school that helped you understand that difficult concept in your courses. Become that person to build trust and a relationship based on respect with your patients.

Patients that research their condition and are on point should be congratulated. Hell, offer them a job. I'm kidding, but that kind of compliment will make them feel better about themselves as well as their new favorite practitioner. So make it a point to ask them and everyone else (friends, family, reps, employees) to let you know about a research site that they utilize. This way, you can do some research and see which sites are credible and offer educated, valuable advice to your patients.

Sometimes a patient is led astray by what they heard from someone or an article that was taken out of context. How do you bring them down gently? Because once someone believes something, it is often hard to change his or her mind on that topic. One solution is to show them your documented proof (journal studies and research). By no means should you blow them off because you are the expert. If they are still hesitant to believe you after all the research you show them, then you might want to tell them to get a second opinion. Sometimes it is okay to agree to disagree, and suggesting they see someone else will let them know you're not focused first on making a sale or on being right.

So the steps here are simple:

1. Ask them to bring in the research. Ask them to give you time to check everything out.
2. Bring in your research at the second visit if you disagree with theirs.
3. Agree to disagree and help them find another provider.

Yes, that's right. You will help them find another provider. There are a lot of psychological aspects to this, but if we keep it simple—you're just being the nice guy or gal. They will remember that and I guarantee that they will still value your opinion on their next medical issue.

A friend of the practice once referred a runner to my clinic who had some serious knee issues. While I was conducting my evaluation, he wanted to let me know that I was the fifth therapist he had seen and also the fourth sports doctor, all for the same problem. I stopped my evaluation and asked him to let me know more about each therapist and doctor he had seen, what they did that worked and what didn't work. We also discussed his understanding of his symptoms.

I listened carefully and respectfully to what he had to say and I advised him on what I have seen through the years. In the end, it came down to the simple fact that he needed to cut down on the number of marathons he ran and trained for each year to let his body heal. He did not accept this as an answer. I agreed to disagree and referred him to an excellent knee surgeon to give him the options he was seeking. That same patient has referred more runners to me due to my honesty and ability to think differently than my colleagues than any other.

Sometimes you can only guide them. In the end, the patient has the final say about their health.

For more information and free bonuses, please visit ,

www.privatepracticebusinessacademy.com.

Chapter 31 – Invest In Your Second Education: Running A Business

The majority of clients that I have consulted with all have higher degrees. As a matter of fact, they all have so many letters behind their names that I don't know what they all mean. Let's take Stephanie, for example. Stephanie hired me to consult on opening up her private practice. I was a bit shocked that someone so young, not age-wise, but in her career, wanted to hire a consultant. So I commended her for this.

As we spoke about her goals and vision, I saw that she was tainted by her experience with her previous employer. Stephanie had worked as a staff therapist for two years. In these two years, she knew that she could do a better job at treating her former employer's patients than the doctor she worked for. She told me that she wanted to be the best clinician in town and that meant to her that she needed to learn more. So Stephanie spent those two years completing certifications and her doctoral degree. She spent a lot of money on her education. You bet. But her patients didn't know the difference.

You see, Stephanie added all of those letters to her signature, but her clients never knew that. Then she approached her employer and asked for a raise. Her employer told her reimbursements were down and she could not afford to pay her more. She did offer to pay for her continuing education courses because she thought that Stephanie enjoyed taking classes.

Stephanie was furious. So she did what a lot of people think they should do: she started her own practice.

Mistake #1 – I told Stephanie that she should not have burned bridges. Her employer was probably not lying to her; running a business is hard, and many doctors are not as good at business as they are at treating patients.

Mistake #2 – Stephanie spent a lot of money on education to add more letters behind her signature, but Mr. and Mrs. Jones do not know what those letters mean.

Mistake #3 – She did not invest in a business education and did not study how her employer ran her company.

Stephanie, like many private practice owners, believes that if she is the best, people will find her and come to her and the floodgates of referrals will open. If you believe this, please stop reading this book. As a matter of fact, just throw it out. Because you have to be willing to be open minded. Let me teach you what experience and observing others has taught me.

No matter how many letters you have behind your name, the average Joe does not care about any of that. What do you think they care about? Let's brainstorm. If you went to a doctor's office and were in a lot of pain, what is the first thing that you would want that doctor to do? That's right: you would care less about where the doctor went to school or what letters they had behind their signature and more about feeling better, and fast.

Now, I know with what my critics are saying: "I check to see where my doctor went to school and what their credentials are." Fine, I agree, but again, if you are in pain and you are referred to a doctor that treats that specific thing, do you care at that moment if he did an extra course or received a certificate in xyz medical training? But that is just one part.

Let's go back. I said you were referred to this doctor. But what if you didn't have a referral. What is your next step? Yellow Pages, Internet, call your friends, look at your insurance company's list? How do you get attention? How do you stand out in the crowd? How do you become the go-to provider? This is why it is so important to invest in your business education.

Being the best is good, but letting people know you are the best is still incredibly valuable. If you don't have the right tools to get noticed and stand out from the crowd, then don't open your own private practice. Because you will be bankrupt in six months. So how do you invest in yourself to become a better businessperson?

Today's Prescription
Well, for one, you are reading this book. It is a good first step. Second, if you hire a consultant to coach you, which I personally believe in, it will take you to the next level faster and will be more effective than anything else. Imagine if working with a coach could help you earn more in your first year of private practice as you would after five years of trying to figure it out for yourself. A coach that helps you to keep from reinventing the wheel is worth whatever you can afford, and more.

Another constructive thing would be to go sales and marketing seminars outside your industry. This is probably one of the most important things you can do. If you wished you lived in New York City so that you could find me, don't fret. I run a very successful monthly coaching program to help entrepreneurs like yourself get your feet wet. Go to **www.privatepracticebusinessacademy.com** to learn more.

Insider tip: Get involved in masterminding, as Napoleon Hill encourages. (If you don't know who Napoleon Hill is, please go to Amazon and order Think And Grow Rich. It is one of the best business books ever written.) Now back to the topic of masterminding. When you are in a room with like-minded individuals collaborating to increase your business and theirs, that is masterminding. When I joined my first mastermind five years ago, I was exited to find and speak to people that thought like me. None of my close friends or family were knowledgeable about or much interested in my ideas about business. It was a tremendous joy to find others just like me. People that enjoyed listening to my ideas (if you are married, you will understand the inside joke with this), and people I could get even better ideas from.

So please, invest in your second education (your business education) over getting one more letter or certification. This will help you invest in and grow your business.

For more information and free bonuses, please visit,

www.privatepracticebusinessacademy.com.

Chapter 32 – What Is Your Online Reputation?

Just like in the real world, your reputation as a provider means everything. In the good old days, if a disgruntled patient were upset with you, they would badmouth you to their friends and family. In the information-centric, 4G world, everyone goes online. And that same disgruntled patient will now write you up on a review site. The big ones like Yelp and Citysearch are the main ones, and there might be something else by the time you read this book.

I have had my own issues with online reputation. But before I get into that story, I want to tell you about a recent dentist visit. Knowing I do some consulting for healthcare practitioners and that I work in the industry, he wanted to pick my brain while I was in the chair. Trapped audience. And I really wouldn't say no to a man with a drill in his hand. He was wondering if I had seen a drop off in business recently. It was the summer and business usually slows down then (unless you prepare beforehand).

Inside tip: Know your slow periods throughout the year and prepare for them by marketing beforehand and creating programs that run at that time. **For more information and free bonuses, please visit www.privatepracticebusinessacademy.com.**

I told him that we were a bit slower than normal and I had to ask, how slow was he? The doctor mentioned that he was down 40%. I almost fell out of my chair. What? How was this possible? He was even more frightened by my reaction. I told him we should go through his systems, check his follow up and marketing plan for the year as well as the projected income. Everything looked great. But in May, he had a sharp decline. So I did some back-end research. I just googled him. And all of my questions were answered.

An ex-employee wrote him a horrible review on multiple sites (without using his real name, but some of the information on the review was only privy to the staff). The doctor explained to me that he had fired the review writer because he was often late and not doing a good job. Regardless of the reason, the ex employee went on a rampage and posted comments from multiple emails for one month. He posted for the month of May. Without professional intervention, the doctor's dental practice was doomed.

He wanted to know if he should he hire a reputation management team. I told him the answer was clearly yes. They are quite expensive, but not as expensive as losing 40% of his business.

Today's Prescription

Inside tip - The solution to online reputation problems: You must respond to all accusations. There are always two sides to every story. You will have a very small chance of getting a poor review removed, so another solution is to get all of your great patients to start posting positive comments. And why not also have your staff post? Is this unethical? Is it unethical that his former employee did this? Fight fire with fire. Ask family and friends to post as well.

Online reputation is very important. People want to see who you are. If they see a strike against you, they might just keep searching for another provider. Don't give them that chance. Telling your side of the story might at least make someone think, "Well, at least they were honest." So monitor your reputation monthly; the quicker the response, the better. If bad online reviews are already sapping your business, look into professional reputation management help immediately.

For more information, please visit www.privatepracticebusinessacademy.com.

Chapter 33 – Make Sure They Can Find You

"All the bells and whistles in the world, but I couldn't find their address." This was a comment from one of the patients in my client's physical therapy practice. Dr. Westfield had spent $15,000 on his website. I must admit that I was a bit amazed at everything that he had on there. So you can imagine my surprise when I surveyed his patients and found out that they could not find his address on the site. Worse, when they googled him, his old address popped up. This is a great example of poor implementation across the board. Assess your site today to make sure people can find you. The tips below will help you.

Today's Prescription

Tip #1 – First things first: make sure your address and phone number are on your homepage on the top right. Why the top right? Because there is something called the "f-pattern." The f-pattern is the most common pattern in tracking a person's vision. They look at the top of the site from left to right. Then they look down the left side, and just above the middle they track their eyes to the right again, then finally look down the bottom left until they reach the bottom of the page. So you can see, this movement traces the shape of the letter "f."

The best place to keep your contact information is the top right-hand corner of the site. That's where people will look for it, and if it's not there, they may not bother looking for wherever else you might have put it.

Tip #2 – Next, make sure you are listed on Google Local. This is basically the Yellow Pages of the 21st century, and Google can bring extra relevance to your business if used correctly. Google Local is an easy way for patients that live or work in your area to find you. With more and more people using their phones for quick and easy access, being listed on Google Local is the cheapest and greatest return on time invested in setting it up. The setup time is less than five minutes!

These two small tips can increase your business by 10% of yearly revenue. And that is huge. My bonus tip is next (I generally save this one only for those that tell me that they already did #1 and #2). I know some marketing experts say to blanket your neighborhood with postcards and flyers and that will help your business. But tip #3 has that beat hands–down: SIGNAGE. Most businesses have a sign outside. Most signs look like this: **"Insert Name Here" Physical Therapy**.

Here are some examples of names you might see, and I apologize if I offend anyone. I have to admit that I was guilty of the same thing when I first started.

- Excel
- Healing hands
- Aspire
- Excellent
- Peak
- Smile
- "Your last name" + profession
- Etc.

What do we really learn from the names above? That you're good, or that you want to help? All of them are creative, but how will they help your patients find you? They won't. How will your patients find you? Through referrals you got from doctors, family and friends? Years ago, this was the way to do it. Times have changed. The concept behind this book is to get patients through the front door.

Today's Prescription (2)

Now, if you are opening a practice today, my best advice for you is to make it easy for your audience to find you. Put your location or your exact target audience in the name of your company. If you are in a small town and someone already took the name of the town, that's okay; your other option is to create a name of the exact target audience that you want to work with, for example:

1. Great Falls Physical Therapy & Sports Rehabilitation
2. Confident Smiles Dentistry
3. West Hanover Sports Medicine Group

Two of these examples had a location in their names and one had their tagline. But this tagline described exactly what they can provide. Easily accessible and simple for the patient to google it.

The concept here is to make it easy for your target audience to find you. Keeping them in the name of your practice not only becomes the natural choice in someone's brain, but if we also think in terms of keyword searches on the Internet, this will make you land on page one. And that is without doing a whole lot of SEO work.

If you don't know who your target audience or ideal patient is, please visit **www.privatepracticebusinessacademy.com** to schedule a phone consultation with me today.

Chapter 34 – Bribe The Significant Other

If I came to your office (and this is going to be true for internists, physical therapists, dentists and dermatologists, etc.) and we ran a report to see if your audience was predominantly male or female (besides the obvious professions), the numbers always show that more females visit doctors' offices and not just more, but more also more frequently. Women in general will visit a doctor's office at the first sign of any adverse symptoms. Men, on the other hand (and I am guilty of this), will go with the "let's see what happens maybe it will go away naturally" approach.

This is especially true for dental practices that I have consulted for. Dr. Ramirez had two dental practices in south Florida and he was spending a ton of marketing dollars to get patients in the office. I met Dr. Ramirez and he hired me for a one-day business exposure session. So we started with the basics. Who was his target market and who was already coming into his practice? His stats clearly showed 82% female and 18% male, so I literally cut his marketing dollars in half.

Instead of throwing the big blanket out there for everyone, we narrowed down his net to women aged forty-five to sixty. And then we put an in-house referral program in place, telling all those female patients that if they brought their significant others in for a check up, they would receive a gift card to the spa that was located a few blocks away.

Dr. Ramirez's numbers tripled overnight. Not only did his current marketing bring in more females, but the in-house marketing increased his bottom line by 13% net profit. This 13% was because he didn't spend marketing money on the referral program. In fact, the gift card was such a great incentive he formed a great relationship with the owner of the spa.

Remember, you can never have too much influence over a prospective patient, so whatever means are available to you to convince them to join and to keep coming, by all means, use it.

Think of an ethical bribe to offer to satisfied patients in order to push them to refer their significant other to you.

Today's Prescription

Your homework assignment is to create a database of your patients' family members and emergency contacts (which I believe every doctor's office gets) and do a promotion for those emergency contacts.

Yes, I know that most emergency contacts do not live with the patient. But this is fine. Create the list, and then send an email to your patient offering them a gift if they refer their emergency contact today. Your satisfied patients have much more influence over their friends and family than you do; leverage that influence to your advantage. I think I saw the little light go on in your head and a smile come across your face.

For more information and free bonuses, please visit,

www.privatepracticebusinessacademy.com.

Chapter 35 – Join Now!

Every trade, profession or occupation has an association you can join, and it is no different for the medical and rehabilitation community. Don't get me wrong; these associations are not perfect, but neither are you. For years, I was not a part of the APTA, the association for physical therapists. I was disgruntled, angry and downright pissed off that they were not doing enough for physical therapists. But the older I became and the more mature of a practitioner I became, the more I realized that no one is perfect. And they are trying to fight against bigger lobbies with deeper pockets. Many people have many complaints, but if you are not a part of the solution, then you are part of the problem.

The two keys to getting the most out of an association are (1) look at the dues as an investment instead of a cost, and (2) remember that you have to get involved to get value.

To get value from an association, you must attend the events and volunteer on projects that put you in front of more people. The more people you are in front of, the more people will know about your business. And soon, either the person you speak in front of, or their family, or a friend will schedule an appointment to your office or clinic. Also, enjoy the social interaction. 90% of practitioners never get to leave the office. You will be amazed what happens when you leave the office. Trust me, it won't break down (hopefully).

Once, I sent a physical therapy private practice owner to cooking classes. Yes, a cooking class. He was in the room with forty other participants. By the end of the preparation, everyone was making conversation and at least half knew he was a PT. In about forty-eight hours, several people from the class scheduled appointments at his office. The PT soon became a member of the cooking club and he not only generated referrals, but also went on a few dates because of it as well.

Today's Prescription

The moral of the story is to be a joiner. Join associations, clubs, and after-work activities. Join and become and active member of things outside of your practice. Who knows: you might even enjoy it. Take the first step and join my community on Facebook just for private practice business owners

For more information and free bonuses, please visit,

www.privatepracticebusinessacademy.com.

Chapter 36 – Strategic Partnerships

Many offices see their patients as just that: patients that need help. Most medical facilities care, but not so much that they consider the patient a partner in their business. But let's face the facts: patients are the lifeblood of your business or any medical practice. And most patients don't care about you until they know how much you care about them.

The advantage we as medical professionals have above every other industry it that is in our nature to care and it is easy for us to show how much we care.

So try to be different in your practice. Try to see patients as partners that will help your practice become more profitable and productive. Make sure your relationships are positive for everyone. It is important that your patients know you are not taking advantage of them. A great example of this is Ivan Candelaria, PT ATC.

Ivan has been practicing Certified Athletic Trainer for years and he has developed relationships with many athletes, high school football players in particular. He was not only their medical and fitness counsel, he was also their friend. Those same kids went to college and played more. He continued to be the go-to person for any medical advice as they matured. So much so that the parents would request that their child be seen and treated by Ivan personally. Ivan did not disappoint. He worked long hours and made sure to make strategic partnerships with the students, their families and healthcare professionals. What happened to those high school and college football players? Well, some play in the NFL, and guess what? He is still their go-to guy because of those partnerships.

This can be done in every medical industry, not just in physical therapy and fitness. Dental and chiropractic massage all have access to high school and college patients. This is just one example of what worked. There are thousands more. Build a good relationship with your patients and let them know you will help them if they can help you. It is 50/50, almost like a marriage.

For more information and free bonuses, please visit ,

www.privatepracticebusinessacademy.com.

Chapter 37 – Intentional Relationships

Let's build on the last chapter in which we spoke of strategic partnerships and how their nature leads to and builds relationships with patients. So what are intentional relationships? Intentional relationships are just that: they are relationships that did not happen purely out of coincidence.

My friend Mike Costes, DDS, spoke to me during a mastermind meeting and mentioned how he was working on building long-term relationships with doctors in a nearby town by playing golf at that town's golf course for over a year. He mentioned that after some time, there were chance meetings on the course or in the locker room. But when there was a charity drive, Dr. Costes made sure that he was a part of it and soon the physicians' group invited Dr. Costes to be a part of an additional joint venture they were working on.

This never would have happened if he hadn't spent the time, effort and money to consistently work on an intentional relationship that Dr. Costes realized would benefit his practice immensely.

Lets use the predator and prey analogy from the animal kingdom. When you are searching for your prey, you will have to do your research. Who will be an added benefit or value to your clinic? Who can increase your revenue with their expertise? Once you know your prey, you go into hunt mode. You spend the time and show up at different events and functions. Be a value added; don't be a stalker. I'm asking you to add value to their lives and to their practices.

I guarantee that they will notice, from the very small things to the big. People are always watching and observing. And when the time comes, you will react and you will be victorious like a lion in the jungle. I hope this analogy helped you. I must have watched a lot of Animal Planet last night before I wrote this, but the concept is still apt. Make it a point to connect with those that will be able to complement your business and you will wonder how you survived before you met them.

For more information and free bonuses, please visit,

www.privatepracticebusinessacademy.com.

Chapter 38 – Don't Be So Modest

I want the whole world (or at least everyone in the country) to know how good you are. I want you to brag about it and then brag some more. Will Rogers said, "Get someone else to blow your horn and the sound will travel twice as far." If you have made intentional relationships and it is working out for you, make sure to brag about them to everyone, and I mean everyone. The word will get back to the other doctors you have befriended. They will hear about how much you talk about them. When they talk to you or call you to thank you, make sure to ask them to please return the favor. All it takes is for someone else to talk about how great your services are to have a huge impact on your practice. This leverages the power of someone else's network. Imagine the benefit in referrals if you could leverage the networks of two, three, four or even more other private practitioners.

Even better than word of mouth, ask if they would do a testimonial for you. If can be written or in the form of a video, and this is how you become a national celebrity. Because once the video gets on YouTube or on a website, countless people will watch it and they can spread the word virtually.

Another example is to talk to everyone about how you helped someone. Talk to everyone you meet, especially if you helped a local celebrity. People like to see and hear social proof. When you brag about helping a local celebrity, it is nothing but amazing how fast the word will spread.

Most healthcare practitioners are modest, and to get them to talk about themselves is a challenge. 98% of healthcare practitioners are modest to the point that they don't want to be recognized for their accomplishments. They feel that when they help someone it is a part of their job. I need to break you of that. I need to show you that word of your success needs to be spread. And in the age of viral media and social sharing, the more you brag, the more people hear. The loudest drum makes the most noise. And in return gets the most referrals.

For more information and free bonuses, please visit,

www.privatepracticebusinessacademy.com.

Chapter 39 – Implement Immediately

I have given you thirty-plus ways of increasing the number of patients that can be attained by your practice. But the key here is implementation. I want you to read a chapter and implement that idea immediately. The ideas can't work until you sit down with your staff, your computer, or your significant other and put them to work. After you've implemented the first idea, commit to implementing one more each day for thirty days.

The more you try, the more patients will flood your business, to the point where you will be forced to open up another practice. No matter how bad things are in your business, you have the ability to make them better. Don't ever give up. Sometimes the changes are minuscule and sometimes they are drastic. Start small and work your way up. You don't have to spend a fortune either.

Remember: you are a healer and it's not your fault that you didn't major in business. But here is the thing: you didn't have to. A lot of the things that I teach here are based on trial and error and human psychology. Sales and marketing are the key components of keeping a business scalable, systemized and sellable, and sales and marketing are all about psychology.

In the end, we all want the same thing. We want a practice that affords us a comfortable lifestyle and along the way we want to help as many people as possible. We want to help them feel better or smile more.

So make sure to re-read some of the chapters again. Underline and highlight. If you need help, I am here just for that. Go to **www.privatepracticebusinessacademy.com** and let me know how I can be of service.

I created The Private Practice Business Academy to be a community of Medical, Wellness, Holistic practitioners. A community that has the ability to teach and learn from different industries what works and what doesn't.

In the end, I want to make sure that all private practitioners are armed with the business sense & knowledge to take their practice to the next level and be successful & live the life you envisioned when you graduated from university.

About The Author

Dr. Joseph Simon is the owner of a thriving physical therapy practice, Manhattan Physical Therapy & co-owner of countless other medical practices. In addition to treating patients and managing his office, he consults with other healthcare businesses to improve their services, get new patients and increase profits. Dr. Joe uses his proven system to help private practices grow and operate more efficiently, allowing doctors to spend more time seeing patients and less time worrying about the bottom line.

Made in the USA
Middletown, DE
29 October 2015